DINO SAFARI

A LEGO® ADVENTURE IN THE REAL WORLD

by Penelope Arlon
and Tory Gordon-Harris

> I've got a bone to pick with you, mister!

■SCHOLASTIC

New York   Toronto   London   Auckland
Sydney   Mexico City   New Delhi   Hong Kong

LEGO® Minifigures show you the world in a unique non-fiction programme.

This levelled reader is part of a programme of LEGO® non-fiction books, with something for all the family, at every age and stage. LEGO non-fiction books have amazing facts, beautiful real-world photos and minifigures everywhere, leading the fun and discovery.

To find out about the books in the programme, visit www.scholastic.co.uk.

Levelled readers from Scholastic are designed to support your child's efforts to learn how to read at every age and stage.

Purple level books include some long sentences, with the inclusion of complex and simple connectives. They also include some challenging vocabulary. Story features such as plot, character and setting are developed with a level of detail. Some Purple books have short chapters to challenge and encourage reading stamina.

Contents

BUILD IT!

Check out the epic building ideas when you see me!

Come on a dinosaur safari with us. Let's see how many dinosaurs we can spot!

I don't like the look of those raptors. I hope that there's nothing bigger out there . . .

Let's find dinos!

It's millions and millions of years ago. There are no houses, no cars, no phones. Our Earth is ruled by the biggest land animals ever – the dinosaurs. Dinosaur explorers need to watch their step.

Let's go! There were 700 kinds of dinosaur. Let's find as many as we can!

I hear that I might be related to the dinos. I wonder if that's true!

The world is full of huge meat-eaters, and they are all hungry. Run! T. rex wants its breakfast!

BUILD IT!

Build a tall tower for the explorers to climb up and watch the dinosaurs from.

I'll keep you safe and show you what I know. Come on, dino spotters!

This probably isn't the best place for me . . .

5

← Monolophosaurus

Meat-eaters

Every day and night in dino world was a food fight. Dinosaurs were either looking for dinner or trying to not be dinner! Meat-eaters had terrible weapons. Huge, razor-sharp teeth crunched through bones like biscuits. Claws tore through tough skin like paper. Smaller dinosaurs were just as deadly. They had speed and brains, too.

Some meat-munchers had teeth that curved backwards to hold prey.

Utahraptor →

I think I can see the point of those . . . yikes!

ER60082

6

Giganotosaurus ➤

◄ Dilophosaurus

Argh! I'm glad that the dinos will be long gone before people arrive.

BUILD IT!

The explorers need somewhere to shelter. Quick, build a safe, dino-proof hideout!

Spinosaurus ➡

Arrgh! Spinosaurus is coming! Jump in the lake!

Think again! Spinosaurus could swim even faster than it could run!

Take a jaw full of terrifying teeth. Take claws that could slash through a bicycle. Add them to a huge, hungry dinosaur. Say hello to Spinosaurus.

It's the biggest predator of all. Spinosaurus's jaws were as long as your mum or dad!

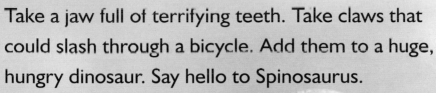

HEARD THIS WORD?

predator: an animal that hunts and eats other animals

Compsognathus was built for speed. I'd better run and save my bacon!

← Compsognathus

A pack of hungry Velociraptors moves around a Protoceratops. The raptors can bring it down only if they work together. They have large claws on their feet, like daggers. Tiny, sharp teeth are ready to tear into Protoceratops's tough skin.

Protoceratops →

Racing raptors! They've formed a pack, but what are they hunting?

Oh, no! The raptors are after Hot Dog Man! Will they catch up?

Let's hope they don't like mustard.

Waaahh!

But Protoceratops fights back. It flicks its thick tail at the raptors. It bites with its sharp beak. Who will win?

Hmm . . . Protoceratops lived in a herd. But even with its friends, I don't think it could beat the raptors.

Velociraptor had a larger brain than other dinos. This was one clever dinosaur.

Velociraptor

Velociraptors could run at 40 miles per hour (64 kph) in short bursts.

Plant-eaters

Some dinosaurs ate only plants. You may think that these herbivores were a calm, friendly bunch. THINK AGAIN! They needed epic battle skills to fight off the meat-eaters. Some of them had horns for stabbing. Club-shaped tails could bash and slam. Thick skulls smashed against one another. Thumb spikes gave nasty pokes.

Look at the large, bony bumps. That sharp beak gives me goosebumps though!

Ankylosaurus

Pachycephalosaurus

◀ Torosaurus

◀ Iguanodon

HEARD THIS WORD?

herbivore: an animal that eats only plants

Skin 6 millimetres thick! My suit of armour is no match for that.

What's the best way to keep safe from a meat-eater?
Have thousands of friends to protect you! Many
plant-eaters lived in herds, or groups. There could be
10,000 dinosaurs in just one herd. If a dinosaur had no
friends – it had to RUN! Gallimimus was one of the
fastest. It could run as fast as a racehorse.

- What's worse than one croc coming for dinner?
- Two crocs coming for dinner!

← Edmontosaurus

Okay, let's see how fast this dino can go. They say that it ran at 40 miles per hour (64 kph)!

Gallimimus →

Dino fight! It's meat-eater against plant-eater. Allosaurus wants a meal. But it's not going to be easy. Stegosaurus has plates on its back. That's not the place to attack. Allosaurus lunges at the neck. In a flash, Stegosaurus swipes its deadly tail at the meat-eater. But Allosaurus is smart and fast. It will figure out how to get its huge jaws around the plant-eater. Who will win?

Allosaurus's short arms didn't help this meat-eater. It needed big, strong arms that punch like mine . . .

← Allosaurus

If Allosaurus won, it had enough food to eat for two weeks.

This is making me hungry How about enough pizza for two weeks? Yum!

← **Stegosaurus**

The best way to not be eaten was to be ENORMOUS. Plant-eaters needed to be REALLY enormous, because meat-eaters were supersize, too. How big was Argentinosaurus? This plant-eater was so big that you couldn't get your arms around its leg! Look up at a three-storey building. That's how tall this dinosaur was!

← Argentinosaurus

At nearly 90,000kg, this dino was about as heavy as a jet.

Imagine all the trees that it trampled and mammals that it squished. Let's fly out of here!

These are t[...]
palaeontolo[...]
Don't breal[...]

BUILD IT!

Think big, and build the most gigantic dinosaur you can imagine.

This vast dino was nearly as long as two tennis courts. That's ace!

19

When peo

thought th

It's not ha

bones we

years, sor

Palaeonto

like jigsaw

HE

Okay! W
pile of
here. Le
you've l
them to

Hmm . .
them to
Where

I think
to bon
dinosau

Build a LEGO® dino world!

It's a minifigure adventure in dinosaur world! Use your stickers to fill the desert landscape. Look out for the Velociraptors! There may be others hiding nearby . . .

Amazing dino words

detective
A person who solves mysteries.

earthquake
A sudden, violent shaking of the Earth.

fossil
A bone, shell, footprint or other trace of an animal or plant from millions of years ago, preserved as rock.

glide
To move through the air smoothly and easily.

hatchling
A baby animal that came out of an egg.

herbivore
An animal that eats only plants.

herd
A group of animals that live or travel together.

meteorite
A piece of rock or metal from space that lands on Earth.

palaeontologist
A scientist who studies fossils to learn about plants and animals that lived a long time ago.

predator
An animal that hunts and eats other animals.

prey
An animal that is hunted and eaten by another animal.

safari
A trip to see wild animals in their natural surroundings.

skull
The set of bones in the head that protects the brain.

©2016 LEGO

©2016 LEGO

I'm going to get my buns out of here before those dinos see me!

Dino names

Allosaurus
AL-oh-SOR-uhs

Ankylosaurus
ANG-kuh-loh-SOR-uhs

Argentinosaurus
AHR-juhn-TEE-noh-SOR-uhs

Compsognathus
komp-SAH-nay-thuhs

Deinonychus
dye-NAH-nik-uhs

Dilophosaurus
dye-LOH-fuh-SOR-uhs

Edmontosaurus
ed-MON-tuh-SOR-uhs

Gallimimus
gal-uh-MYE-muhs

Giganotosaurus
JAI-gan-oh-tuh-SOR-uhs

Iguanodon
ig-WAH-nuh-don

Maiasaura
MYE-uh-SOR-uh

Microraptor
MYE-kroh-RAP-tur

Monolophosaurus
MON-oh-loh-foh-SOR-uhs

Pachycephalosaurus
pak-ee-SEF-uh-loh-SOR-uhs

Protoceratops
proh-toh-SER-uh-tops

Spinosaurus
SPYE-noh-SOR-uhs

Stegosaurus
STEG-uh-SOR-uhs

Therizinosaurus
THER-uh-ZEE-noh-SOR-uhs

Torosaurus
TOR-oh-SOR-uhs

T. rex
TEE reks

Utahraptor
YOO-tah-RAP-tur

Velociraptor
vuh-LOH-suh-RAP-tur